Once upon a time, in the colorful land of Oopsieville, there lived a little boy named Benny. Benny had big floppy ears and rounded rosy cheeks

He loved running around
and exploring the neighborhood
with his friends.

One sunny day, Benny and his friends decided to have a picnic by the neighborhood sparkling stream.

Each friend brought something special to share. Benny had a sweet tooth so he decided to bake carrot cupcakes with his mother's help.

But, oh dear, Benny was so excited that he accidentally mixed up the sugar with salt! Can you believe it?!

SALT
SALT
SUGAR

When the friends took
a bite of Benny's cupcakes,
they all made funny faces.

Some giggled, some stuck their tongues out, and some even pretended to do a little dance.

Benny felt a bit sad. But then, he remembered whathis wise grandma always said, "Mistakes are like sprinkles in the recipe of life — they make it more interesting!"
ORANGE

And so, Benny determined
to turn things around!
Benny suggested they have a
cupcake decorating contest.

Luckily, Benny's mom had some plain cup cakes she brought to the stream from a batch she mixed with sugar.

Each friend got to create their own cupcake masterpiece using the extra colorful toppings, sprinkles, and even a few chocolate chips Benny brought in his picnic basket.

The picnic turned into a laughter-filled, sprinkle-covered adventure!

As the sun began to set, Benny
thought about something important.
You know," he said with a big smile, "
making mistakes is okay! It's how we learn
and make things better and sometimes fun!

His friends nodded in agreement.
They all did Benny's favorite dance,
singing ooh yeah!, ooh yeah.

Ooh yeah
Ooh yeah
ORANGE JUICE

They all agreed that Benny's cupcakes, despite the mix-up, were the most delicious because they were made with love and a sprinkle of laughter.
Ooh yeah
Ooh yeah

And so, in Oopsieville, everyone learned that mistakes were not the end of the world — they were the beginning of something new and exciting.

From that day forward, whenever someone made a little oopsie, they would just say, "Oopsie-daisy!"
Oopsie-daisy

Everyone in Oopsieville learnt to turn mistakes into an adventure.

Just like Benny and his friends did on that sunny day by the sparkling stream.

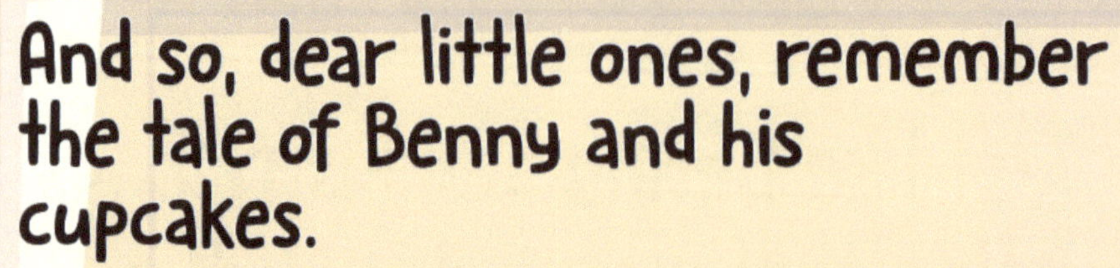

And so, dear little ones, remember the tale of Benny and his cupcakes.

Mistakes happen, but they can lead to the most wonderful surprises if you sprinkle them with a positive attitude and a dash of fun!

The End